Temple Building:

Realigning The Body of Christ

Tfifany Moore Palmer

Basar Publishing

Temple Building: Realigning the Body of Christ

Copyright © 2015 by Tfifany Moore Palmer

All rights reserved. No part of this book may be reproduced or transmitted in any form or by any means without written permission from the author, except in the case of brief quotations embodied in critical articles or reviews.

All Scripture quotations, unless otherwise indicated, are taken from the King James Bible Version.

ISBN **978-1-942013-73-0**

Printed in USA by 48HrBooks

Cover Design: PF Dezigns

Editors: Montez Dove, Leslyn Johnson, Donna Moore Wesby

Dedication

Without God, I can do nothing! He placed the mandate to write this project in my heart and he placed the people in my path to encourage me along the way.

To Mrs. Violet Hickson, a true woman of worship. I thank you for challenging me to continually seek God by asking, "What's the Word?" Many of your "Hallway Sermons" inspired me to listen to God and write THIS vision.

To Minister Eagle Stacy Lloyd, a true Proverbs 27:17 friend. I love you like a sister and I know you love me the same.

To my sister and biggest cheerleader, Donna Moore Wesby, thank you for always cheering me on!

To my student, mentee, and friend, Leslyn Johnson. Thank you for coming through in the clutch!

To my Boaz, Bernard Palmer. I thank you for always listening to my thoughts, fears and praise reports. Thank you for making me write even when I felt I had nothing to say. Thank you for clarifying the jumbled words for me. And, most of all, thank you for never degrading my dream. You even put your own dreams on the back burner so that you could support mine, and for that, I love you to life!

And, to all those prophets who sit quietly in church pews, trying to be good little parishioners Sunday after Sunday, this book is for you!

Contents

Introduction i
1-The Body 1
2-The Head 9
                    Eyes, Ears, Mouth, Nose
3- The Shoulders 27
                           Arms, Hands
4- The Hips 41
5- The Knees 49
6- The Feet 55
7- Muscles, Ligaments & The Blood 65
8-The Body Re-Aligned 71
Building The Temple 79
Temple Dedication Prayer 80
References 81
About the Author 83

Introduction

Imagine this:

Early Christmas morning your children wake you up to go see the wonderful gifts left under the tree. It seems they spend just moments tearing through the presents they have been anxiously anticipating all year long. After they have completely littered your family room with empty boxes, tissue paper, wrapping paper and bows, they turn to you and politely say, "I don't want these gifts," and walk out of the room.

How would that make you feel? You would feel rejected. You would probably think your children were spoiled and ungrateful. You might want to scream at them and punish them for being so rude. There is nothing worse than giving a gift that the receiver will not accept. That deflated feeling you feel is how God feels every time we decide not to use the gifts he has placed within us.

Matthew 25: 14-29

[14] For the kingdom of heaven is as a man travelling into a far country, who called his own servants, and delivered unto them his goods. [15] And unto one he gave five talents, to another two, and to another one; to every man according to his several ability; and straightway took his journey. [16] Then he that had received the five talents went and traded with the same, and made them

other five talents. ¹⁷ And likewise he that had received two, he also gained other two. ¹⁸ But he that had received one went and digged in the earth, and hid his lord's money. ¹⁹ After a long time the lord of those servants cometh, and reckoneth with them. ²⁰ And so he that had received five talents came and brought other five talents, saying, Lord, thou deliveredst unto me five talents: behold, I have gained beside them five talents more. ²¹ His lord said unto him, Well done, thou good and faithful servant: thou hast been faithful over a few things, I will make thee ruler over many things: enter thou into the joy of thy lord. ²² He also that had received two talents came and said, Lord, thou deliveredst unto me two talents: behold, I have gained two other talents beside them. ²³ His lord said unto him, Well done, good and faithful servant; thou hast been faithful over a few things, I will make thee ruler over many things: enter thou into the joy of thy lord. ²⁴ Then he which had received the one talent came and said, Lord, I knew thee that thou art an hard man, reaping where thou hast not sown, and gathering where thou hast not strawed: ²⁵ And I was afraid, and went and hid thy talent in the earth: lo, there thou hast that is thine. ²⁶ His lord answered and said unto him, Thou wicked and slothful servant, thou knewest that I reap where I sowed not, and gather where I have not strawed: ²⁷ Thou oughtest therefore to have put my money to the exchangers, and then at my coming I should have received mine own with usury. ²⁸ Take therefore the talent from him, and give it unto him which hath ten talents. ²⁹ For unto every one that hath shall be given, *and he shall have abundance: but from him that hath not shall be taken away even that which he hath.*

Our God is a giver. He gives us things He intends for us to use. If we do not use those gifts, he will take them away and give them to someone else.

So many believers are stuck in the rut of "pew membership" because of statements that have been made like, "we don't prophesy in the Baptist church" or "deliverance is not for today." If you have a gift that is "not for today" you hide it and pray that God would take it from you in an effort to fit in with the culture of "the church." Churches that do practice the charismatic gifts of the Holy Spirit are labeled "weird" and are thought to be a cult.

But the Bible clearly says in I Corinthians 12:4-11,

> *"There are different kinds of gifts, but the same Spirit distributes them. There are different kinds of service, but the same Lord. There are different kinds of working, but in all of them and in everyone it is the same God at work. Now to each one the manifestation of the Spirit is given for the common good. To one there is given through the Spirit a message of wisdom, to another a message of knowledge by means of the same Spirit, to another faith by the same Spirit, to another gifts of healing by that one Spirit, to another miraculous powers, to another prophecy, to another distinguishing between spirits, to another speaking in different kinds of tongues, and to still another the interpretation of tongues. All these are*

Temple Building: Realigning The Body of Christ

the work of one and the same Spirit, and he distributes them to each one, just as he determines."

Now, if the Holy Spirit gave us the gifts, He intends for us to use them. Who has the right to tell us not to?! The Apostle Paul told Timothy to "fan into flames" the gifts that were imparted and awakened within him. The only way a spark turns into a flame is for it to be exposed to the open air!

God is calling the true believers to expose our gifts! He is requiring us to stop pretending the gift does not exist and become The Body of Christ we are intended to be. Each gift is important, just as each body part is important for The Body to function to its full capacity.

1
~The Body~

"What is the purpose of The Body?" Type this question into a search engine and you will get a plethora of interesting answers, most of which are spiritual. There are numerous scientific theories that try to explain away the miracles of God, such as the thought that humans evolved from apes. But, in my research, I could not find one scientific explanation of the PURPOSE of the human body.

The Holy Bible declares, in Genesis chapter 2 verse 15,

> "And the Lord God took the man, and put him into the Garden of Eden to dress it and keep it." Genesis chapter 1 verse 28 says, "And God blessed them, and God said unto them, be fruitful, and multiply, and replenish the earth, and subdue it: and have dominion over the fish of

Temple Building: Realigning The Body of Christ

the sea, and over the fowl of the air, and over every living thing that moveth upon the earth." (KJV)

The human body was created to be stewards of the Earth. God's design of the human body was in His image and likeness. He told Adam that his purpose was to be fruitful and multiply, take dominion and subdue the earth. God created man, the human body, to take care of His earth. God had dominion of the Heavens and He gave the human dominion of the earth. The purpose of the body is still the same; to move in various directions, lift and carry things that need to go somewhere else, reproduce and facilitate reproduction of the other beings that God made.

God proclaims in Genesis chapter 1 verse 26, "Let us make man in our image, after our likeness…" At first glance, the words image and likeness seem like the same thing. However, the words "image" and "likeness" are two different words in the original text.

"Image" is the Hebrew word "tselem," which can also be interpreted as "an idol." Image, according to merriam-webster.com, is a visual representation of something. So, in making the human body, God made a visual representation of himself. In other words, the human body physically looks and is set up similarly to God's.

Likeness is the Hebrew word "demuwth," which means "appearance." (blueletterbible.com). Likeness in the Merriam Webster dictionary is "the fact or quality of being alike; resemblance; the semblance, guise, or outward appearance of; a portrait or representation. I love the 3rd

~The Body~

definition, a portrait or representation. God created humans to be a representation of Him on the earth.

Being made in God's image and likeness means that we not only are the physical mirror image of our Creator, but we are the spiritual representation of our Creator. He created us with a body, soul and spirit. The spirit is His way of connecting and communing with us. The soul gives us the ability to think and feel, as He also thinks and feels. And the body was given so that we could MOVE.

As a body made in the image and likeness of God, we have to understand that God requires us to not be stagnant. Genesis 1:2 says God moved over the waters. Before the world was created, God MOVED. The great characters of The Bible were people who were not afraid to move. Abraham moved away from his family to develop a prosperous life without the corruption perpetuated by his family. Moses led a movement for forty years! Jesus moved from place to place as he performed healings and miracles. Paul, even shackled, moved throughout the Roman Empire to encourage and edify the growing Christian church. And, Jesus' last commandment to his followers was to "Go!" (Mark 16:15)

Now, this principle of moving and going is very motivational when talking about the individual body, but it is also true of the church body. I Corinthians 12:27 says, "Now you are the body of Christ, and each one of you is a part of it." I Corinthians 6:15a says, "Do you not know that your bodies are members of Christ himself?"

Temple Building: Realigning The Body of Christ

The church cannot perform its calling unless we MOVE. And, so as The Body we are to move. We are to go into the dark places of this earth and work the land so that it begins to flourish and produce good fruit.

In order for the body to move, work the land and produce good fruit, we have to be aware of each body part, its purpose and how it can contribute to the growth, development and movement of the body.

Ephesians 4:11-12; 16 says,

> *"So Christ himself gave the apostles, the prophets, the evangelists, the pastors and teacher to equip his people for works of service, so that the body of Christ may be built up. From him the whole body, joined and held together by every supporting ligament, grows and builds itself up in love, <u>as each part does its work</u>."*

Christ gave His body the structure that if aligned correctly, will create a long lasting stability, strength and ability to GO!

God showed me by his Spirit that the human body is a physical "likeness" or representation of this principle of Spiritual alignment. The head represents the apostle, the shoulders represent the prophets, the hips/pelvis represents the evangelist, the knees represent the pastors and the feet represent the teachers. All other parts of the body extend out of this structure and have been given specific assignments/gifts. I Corinthians 12:12 says, "Just as a body, though one, has many parts, but all its many parts form one body, so it is with Christ."

~The Body~

Verses 15-27 go on to say,

> "Now if the foot should say, "Because I am not a hand, I do not belong to the body," it would not for that reason stop being part of the body. And if the ear should say, "Because I am not an eye, I do not belong to the body," it would not for that reason stop being part of the body. If the whole body were an eye, where would the sense of hearing be? If the whole body were an ear, where would the sense of smell be? But in fact God has placed the parts in the body, every one of them, just as he wanted them to be. If they were all one part, where would the body be? As it is, there are many parts, but one body. The eye cannot say to the hand, "I don't need you!" And the head cannot say to the feet, "I don't need you!" On the contrary, those parts of the body that seem to be weaker are indispensable, and the parts that we think are less honorable we treat with special honor. And the parts that are unpresentable are treated with special modesty, while our presentable parts need no special treatment. But God has put the body together, giving greater honor to the parts that lacked it, so that there should be no division in the body, but that its parts should have equal concern for each other. If one part suffers, every part suffers with it; if one part is honored, every part rejoices with it. Now you are the body of Christ, and each one of you is a part of it."

Today, so many of our churches are out of alignment.

Temple Building: Realigning The Body of Christ

We are allowing the hips to call themselves the knees and they are serving as the head, when they are actually hips, and we've cut our shoulders and arms off all together! The feet are so confused because they don't know what direction to step because the knees, which are actually hips, are trying to be the head, but they don't have eyes, so there is no vision, and the feet cannot walk where the body cannot see!

The word "alignment" cannot be found in the Bible. However, merriam-webster.com defines alignment as "the state of being arranged in a line or in proper position." Proper position! Too many of our church leaders are serving in a capacity in which God did not call them. Furthermore, they do not allow people who were actually called by God to that position to SERVE in that position. We've gotten away from the biblical explanation of gifts and we are now operating in an improper positioning.

Alignment speaks to order. *"Let all things be done decently and in order,"* I Corinthians 14:40. The word "order" in this scripture is the Greek word "taxis," Strong's Concordance number 5021. It means "an arrangement; right order; the post, rank, or position which one holds in civic or other affairs, since this position generally depends on one's talents, experience, resources." Wow! There is an arrangement in the Body of Christ that is based on the talents of each individual part. We have already seen in scripture that "God has placed the parts just as he wanted them to be." When the body parts are placed in their "proper position," the body can carry out its function in excellence.

~The Body~

Now, alignment can be fixed. Praise the Lord! When the alignment is corrected, and we begin to appreciate the gifts the other body parts possess, the body will begin to MOVE again. The body will begin to grow again. And, the body will begin to take the territory for the Kingdom of God.

Let's take a deeper look at the major parts of the body and their purposes and how we can re-align the body and make it fit for service.

2
~The Head~

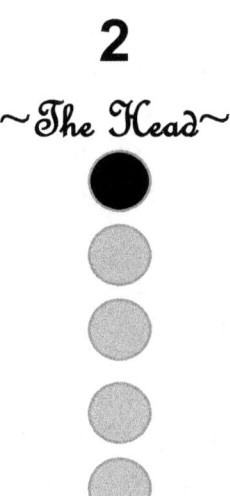

Head, shoulders, knees, and toes! Eyes and ears and mouth and nose, head, shoulders, knees and toes!

Youngsters all over America sing this song daily. This song is a fun way for young people to learn about important body parts. Add the hips, and you have the formula for perfect alignment!

The head is the first and most integral part of the body. The major function of the head is to receive data about your surroundings and make decisions about how to proceed through those surroundings. The head contains the brain, which is the command center for the body. The brain controls conscious movements such as talking and walking, as well as unconscious functions of the body, such as breathing, blinking and heartrate. Everything the body does is filtered through the brain. What is seen, heard, inhaled, felt and eaten is processed in the brain and the brain then decides how the body should react to that information. The brain is a part of the nervous system. The nervous system sends messages to parts of the body to control the voluntary and involuntary actions (movements) that the body makes.

In the Body of Christ, the head represents the apostle.

"And he gave some apostles," Ephesians 4:11.

In the original Greek text of the Bible, apostle is the word "apostolos," Strong's Concordance number g0652. It means "a delegate, specially an ambassador of the Gospel; officially a commissioner of Christ with miraculous powers, he that is sent." The Apostle also functions like the brain in that the apostle organizes the functions of the church body. The Apostle also mobilizes parts of the Body of Christ for specific purposes.

Jesus himself was an Apostle. He says in John chapter 8 verse 18, "I am one who testifies for myself; my other witness is the Father, who sent me." He verifies that he was "sent" by His father, who we know is God, and that God the Father is witness to this fact. Therefore, Jesus was a delegate, an ambassador of the Gospel, which means truth, with miraculous powers, sent by God!

In Ephesians 4:15 Paul declares, *"Instead, speaking the truth in love, we will grow to become in every respect the mature body of him who is the head, that is Christ."* He says it again in Ephesians 5:23, *"… Christ is the head of the church, his body, of which he is the Savior."*

~The Head~

The head includes the brain, ears, nose, eyes and mouth, all strategically placed to accent the apostolic anointing within the body.

In order to truly allow Christ to be head of the body, we must utilize all the faculties of the head the way Jesus would. We must think like Him. We must speak like Him. We must breathe, see and hear like Him too.

Eyes

In the body, the eyes are the vehicle for vision. According to merriam-webster.com, vision is "the ability to see; something you imagine: a picture that you see in your mind; something that you see or dream especially as part of a religious or supernatural experience." The eyes send signals to the brain that tell us whether or not the surroundings are safe. The eyes see obstacles that may be in the body's path and based on that information, the brain tells feet where to lead the body.

The eyes are the conduit to desire as well. When the eye sees something nice looking, desire tells the body to go get it! The concept of desire birthed statements like, "my eyes were bigger than my stomach."

Some of the most powerful agents the enemy uses to peak desire are television, magazines, and the Internet. What we allow the eyes to see can bring darkness or light, and what we allow to enter our eyes dictates whether the body is an agent of darkness or light.

Temple Building: Realigning The Body of Christ

Spiritually, the eyes represent the Watchman anointing. The watchman anointing is extremely important in the Body of Christ. In ancient times, a wall of protection would surround the city. There were gates built into the city's wall that would allow people and cargo to travel in and out of the city. Now, the watchmen would stand on the top of the wall, or in rooms made into the gate especially for the watchmen, so they could see who was coming to visit the city and what the visitors were bringing with them. If the watchmen felt the visitors were friends of the city, they would yell to the gatekeepers to open the gates. If the watchmen felt the visitors were foes, they would sound the alarm to bear arms. The watchmen looked out for danger and provision, just as the eyes look for obstacles in the body's path and objects of desire for the body to have.

2 Kings 9:17-18 (KJV),

> *"And there stood a watchmen on the tower in Jezreel, and he spied the company of Jehu as he came, and said, I see a company. And Joram said, Take an horseman, and send to meet them, and let him say, Is it peace? So there went one on horseback to meet him, and said, Thus saith the king, Is it peace?"* (KJV)

Jesus tells the disciples in Matthew 6:22-23,

> *"The eye is the lamp of the body. If your eyes are healthy, your whole body will be full of light. But if your eyes are unhealthy, your whole body will be full of darkness. If then, the light within you is darkness, how great is that darkness!"*

~The Head~

Let's look at "light" for a minute. The original Greek word interpreted "light" in Matthew 6:22-23 is "lychnos," which means a lamp or candle. According to Thayer's Lexicon (blueletterbible.com), "lychnos" is the prophecies of the Old Testament that reveal Jesus' return and the Holy Spirit that enlightens the prophets of the true meaning of their prophesies (paraphrasing).

Some church bodies are spiritually blind because the leadership will not allow the eyes of the church to function in the way they were intended. Jesus is telling us in Matthew 6 that the eyes are a function of the prophetic gift, working with the gift of discernment, to provide direction for the body, which is the church, which is the function of the apostolic anointing in the body. In modern day churches, the "usher" fulfils the role of watchman AND gatekeeper. And often, the people holding this position are neither prophetic nor discerning.

If we do not have prophetic vision working within our church, the body will not move, thus it will not have life because movement is a function of life. Proverbs 29:18 says, "Without vision, the people perish." Vision in this scripture is defined in the Hebrew as "vision in the night; vision, oracle, prophecy (divine communication)." We as individuals as well as the church must be able to receive "divine communication" from the Lord. Without it, THE BODY WILL PERISH!

But, there is good news… Jesus can heal spiritual blindness!

Luke 18:35-43,

Temple Building: Realigning The Body of Christ

"As Jesus approached Jericho, a blind man was sitting by the roadside begging. When he heard the crowd going by, he asked what was happening. They told him, 'Jesus of Nazareth is passing by.' He called out, 'Jesus, Son of David, have mercy on me!' Those who led the way rebuked him and told him to be quiet, but he shouted all the more, 'Son of David, have mercy on me!' Jesus stopped and ordered the man to be brought to him. When he came near, Jesus asked him, 'What do you want me to do for you?' 'Lord, I want to see,' he replied. Jesus said to him, 'receive your sight; your faith has healed you.' Immediately he received his sight and followed Jesus, praising God. When all the people saw it, they also praised God."

This scripture tells us, individually and as a church body, how to be healed of spiritual blindness.

- First, we see that Jesus is MOVING. The blind man is NOT moving. When the body is spiritually blind, the body does not move. How will the body know where to go without sight?!
- Next, we notice that his detriment was only with his sight. He could still hear. The blind man had been sitting there long enough to know what a crowd passing by sounded like. But this sound was different! It was the sound of praise! When Jesus is visiting, there is always a sound of praise, worship and adoration.
- Healing requires us to "cry out." Even when told to be quit, the blind man cried out to Jesus and got into the flow of praise, prayer and petition that

~The Head~

accompanied Jesus. We have been conditioned as a generation to "suck it up"! People stare at others who are "crying out." We have to stop hindering the "crying out" that is necessary to move with the flow of Jesus.

- God will send help to the body when the body needs it. Sometimes the body needs to rely on other bodies to provide assistance in areas that it is weak. Jesus called for the blind man to be brought to Him. Therefore, the blind man had to rely on someone else's VISION to get to Jesus. Sometimes we cannot get to God on our own; we need the help of others. That's what the early Christian church was all about. When satellite churches were organized in different cities, the Apostles would send teacher, deacons, prophets, etc. to the congregation to help them establish the order that was needed at the time. Being the Body of Christ means we are to help each other move into the vision of the Kingdom.
- Healing also requires us to MOVE from a position of familiarity to a position of faith. The blind man heeded Jesus' call to come. Ultimately, that move of faith was the impetus for his healing.

It is written in Exodus 13:21, *"and the Lord went before them by day in a pillar of a cloud, to lead them the way; and by night a pillar of fire, to give them light to go by day and night."* No matter what the situation, whether bright and shiny or dismal and dark, God is there to show the church the path it should take through prophetic vision and apostolic discernment. God has specifically chosen to speak to us through dreams and visions to give us direction and show us what is to come. We must rely on that vision if we want to be the church Jesus called us to be.

Ears

The ears facilitate hearing of sounds. There are three sections to the ear; the outer ear, the middle ear, and the inner ear. The ears can process multiple sounds at once and they can tell where the sound is coming from and how far away it is. In addition to processing sound, the ears are instrumental in facilitating balance, which helps us MOVE without falling.

God calls to us. When we hear him, we should respond!

"My sheep hear my voice, and I know them, and they follow me," John 10:27 (KJV).

Some churches are spiritually deaf. Being deaf is almost as stifling as being blind. If we do not hear God, we could possibly be lead astray. That spiritual deafness could be caused by disobedience, idolatry or, by ignorance. Most people don't know how to hear God. It's really very simple!

God talks to us through his Word. When you purpose to read the Bible, God speaks to you. Every day that you read the word of God something new will leap off the page at you, and cause your life to change in a positive way.

God also talks through the preached word. I often take notes on preached messages and read those notes

~The Head~

throughout the week. Sometimes, when I go back to those notes months or years later, I receive a fresh word for my current situation. God is not a respecter of persons. What he does for me, he will do for you!

God also speaks through his prophets. If a prophet releases a word to you and you are not accustomed to hearing from the Lord through a prophet, pray for God's direction and he will help you determine what to do with that word. The word may be for a time to come, so write it down and come back to it later. But, whatever you do, don't dismiss it! Acts 3:23 says that "every soul that does not hear the prophet will be destroyed."

Then, you may hear the voice of God in your spirit man. I have rarely heard God as the deep voice spoken to Moses in the movies! Most of the time when I hear God in my spirit, he sounds like an older, more mature me! It's easy to confuse that voice with your own. It's okay to test what you are hearing until you are more familiar with God's voice. Gideon did (Judges 6).

Those who hear and obey the calling of God will receive the following:
- blessings (Proverbs 8:34 and Revelation 1:3)
- life (Deuteronomy 8:3, Isaiah 55:1,3 and John 5:25)
- faith (Romans 10:17)
- consolation (Job 21:2)
- declaration (Job 13:17)
- wisdom (Psalm 8:33 and Proverbs 19:20)
- fear of the Lord and repentance (Deuteronomy 13:11; 19:20)

- healing (Psalm 51:8 and Matthew 13:15)
- relationship with Jesus (Luke 8:21)
- peace (Psalm 85:8)
- love and direction (Psalm 143:8)

If you or your church is lacking in any of the above, check your hearing! The apostolic anointing in your temple, individually and collectively, will hear the sound and work with the eyes and nose to determine what the sound is, where it is coming from, and how far away it is from the body. If the sound is of the Lord, the apostolic anointing will determine if the word is a now word or a future word for the body. If, however, the sound is not coming from the Lord, the body will still respond according to what it hears. It is important to know the sound of the Lord so the body can move in the righteous way, on the righteous path.

Mark 4:9 says, *"And he said unto them, He that hath ears to hear, let him hear."* Let God heal your hearing ears, individually and corporately. Allow the word of God to come forth from those in your congregation who hear him. Hear and obey the voice of God today and be blessed!

Mouth

The mouth essentially has two functions, allow food to enter the body and allow words and air to exit the body. Most obviously, the mouth is used in the first phase in the digestive system. Food enters the body through the mouth, it is then chewed by the teeth into smaller pieces for the body to digest, and the tongue pushes the food into the throat, where it travels to the next phase of digestion.

~The Head~

In addition to aiding the digestive system, the tongue is the muscle that facilitates taste. The tongue has thousands of buds on its surface that send messages to the brain about the taste of an object. Even if the eyes cannot see the object being eaten, the tongue, working with the nose, can discern what is being eaten.

We saw with the eyes that gates are built into the walls of the city to allow people to enter and exit the city. Because the mouth allows things to enter and exit the body, the mouth can be considered a gate of the body. In the body of Christ, the mouth is part of the functions of the apostolic anointing. The apostle knows that "death and life are in the power of the tongue," so what comes into and what exits the body through the mouth must be carefully considered.

"Whoso keepeth his mouth and his tongue keepeth his soul from troubles," Proverbs 21:23 (KJV).

Food is often representative of the preached word.

"And I, brother, could not speak unto you as unto spiritual, but as unto carnal, even as unto babes in Christ. I have fed you with milk, and not with meat: for hitherto ye were not able to bear it, neither yet now are ye able," I Corinthians 3:1-2.

When we are young in the faith, the body can only digest milk. The nutrients in milk are vital to the growth and development of the body! Spiritual milk is the simple message of repentance and salvation, the message John the Baptist and Jesus taught in the beginning of his ministry. Milk is knowledge of God's power. Some people have very thorough knowledge of God's word but do not know how to apply it.

Temple Building: Realigning The Body of Christ

Knowledge comes from reading the word of God and hearing the word of God. The person who has knowledge knows the bible stories, but does not understand yet how the stories apply to their daily walk.

As the body grows and the functions of the body become more precise, the body can begin to digest denser foods, like bread. Bread would represent understanding. Understanding is revelation behind the word of God. I've read the whole Bible several times and every time I read it, I receive a fresh revelation that I did not discern before. Can you relate? Understanding/Revelation helps you see beyond the written word and discern the true reason that particular story is in his word.

The Word of God is often described in the Bible as bread or water. John describes Jesus as the Word (John 1:1-5). And Jesus describes himself in John chapter 6 verse 51 as the bread of life, "I am the living bread which came down from heaven: if any man eat of this bread, he shall live forever; and the bread that I will give is my flesh, which I will give for the life of the world." But, bread can be bad for the body as well. "Thou shalt eat no leavened bread with it; seven days shalt thou eat unleavened bread therewith, even the bread of affliction…," Deuteronomy 16:3 (KJV). And Jesus warned the disciples about the leavened bread of the Pharisees and Sadducees. "*[6]Then Jesus said unto them, Take heed and beware of the leaven of the Pharisees and of the Sadducees.[11] How is it that ye do not understand that I spake it not to you concerning bread, that ye should beware of the leaven of the Pharisees and of the Sadducees? [12]Then understood they how that he bade them not beware of the leaven of bread, but of the doctrine of the Pharisees and of the Sadducees."*

Sometimes, a messenger of the word can focus so much on the knowledge of God, they forget that the knowledge is supposed to nourish the body. The leaven of the Pharisees and Sadducees is a doctrine of greed, compromise and hypocrisy. The Pharisees and Sadducees were religious leaders who spun (leaven) the Word of God (bread) to keep the people bound by rules and laws they themselves were not even abiding by, in an effort to pacify the Roman rulers. The Pharisees and Sadducees were trying to keep the Body from MOVING. Jesus warned them about this "leaven" because of what is said in Galatians 5:9, "A little leaven leaveneth the whole lump." Only a little belief in this unsound doctrine creates a spirit of disbelief throughout the whole church body!

"Therefore let us keep the feast, not with old leaven, neither with the leaven of malice and wickedness; but with the unleavened bread of sincerity and truth," I Corinthians 5:8. (KJV)

Unleavened bread is pure, undefiled and righteous. It does not glory in itself, but it only glorifies God, in all three of his forms. Unleavened bread is Jesus, the perfect sacrifice for our sin. It is the bread of life, the nourishment the body needs to grow and GO!

And, when the body is fully matured, it can digest the densest food of all, meat. The goal of every believer and church body should be the ability to digest meat!

Temple Building: Realigning The Body of Christ

The website medicaldaily.com lists three benefits of eating meat. The first reason for eating meat is that it is rich in protein which builds and repairs the body's muscles and tissue, strengths the immune system, and is good for the overall health of the body. The second reason the website sites for eating meat is that it is rich in iron, which aid in the production of hemoglobin to transport oxygen to the body through the blood; zinc, which is instrumental in tissue formation and higher metabolism of energy; and selenium, which breaks down extra fat in the body. The third benefit of eating meat is that it is a great source of the vitamins A, B and D, which strengthens the skin, eyes, teeth and bones, as well as promotes mental health and maintain excellent performance of the central nervous system.

Meat represents the ability to not only know the word of God, not only understand the word of God, but now apply the word of God. Spiritually, the Body of Christ relies on wisdom to apply the knowledge and understanding of the word of God. *Proverbs 24:3 says, "Through wisdom is an house builded; and by understanding it is established."* Like meat, wisdom is essential to building the body as a temple/house of the Lord.

Proverbs 9:10 says, "The fear of the Lord is the beginning of wisdom: and the knowledge of the holy is understanding." Knowledge, understanding and wisdom are always connected as sources of spiritual food in the Bible, just as milk, bread and meat are connected as sources of food for our natural bodies.

~The Head~

Jesus proclaims in Matthew 4:4 that *"man shall not live by bread alone, but by every word that proceedeth out of the mouth of God."* Every word is either milk, bread or meat. Allow the body to experience the whole truth of God's word which is found in the knowledge, understanding and wisdom thereof.

Nose

The nose is the facilitator of the sense of smell. When air comes into the nose, small hairs in the nasal cavity tell the brain what is "in the air."

Smell is related to the gift of spiritual discernment. To determine if food is fresh or rotten, you smell it! The same is true for the gift of discernment.

The Hebrew word for discernment is "Nakar." It means to recognize, acknowledge, know, observe, notice, perceive and understand. The nose receives an order and filters the odor through the brain to recognize what that odor is and where it is most likely coming from. The gift of discernment functions in much the same way. The person with the gift of discernment will observe a person's actions and recognize the true motives of the person, even if the person has said something completely different.

After recently meeting someone, people with a gift of discernment will say things like, "I have a bad/good feeling about that person." And, usually, the initial feeling the discerner had is found to be true as time passes.

There are three functions of spiritual discernment, discerning of human spirits, discerning of demonic spirits and discerning of angelic spirits. I Corinthians 12:10 says that the Spirit gave this gift to the Body. Hebrews chapter 5 says that those who have this gift to discern between good and evil are ready to eat meat! And when King Solomon was praying for wisdom in I Kings 3, he said, "Give therefore thy servant an understanding heart to judge thy people that I may discern between good and bad…" God granted King Solomon's request and He will do the same for you and The Body of which you are a part.

Mind

The body is a tri-part being comprised of body, soul and spirit. The mind is part of the three components of the soul, along with will and emotions. Merriam-Webster.com defines the mind as "the part of a person that thinks, reason, feels and remembers." The mind, the ability to think and reason, can be influenced by desire, which is influenced by the information that enters the eye, ear, mouth and nose gates.

> Ephesians 2:3, *"Among whom also we all had our conversation in times past in the lusts of our flesh, fulfilling the desires of the flesh and of the mind; and were by nature the children of wrath, even as others."*

~The Head~

This causes the body to act in worldly ways and flip flop between being a righteous Son of God and a follower of the kingdom of darkness.

> James 1:8, *"A double minded man is unstable in all his ways."*

The double minded man has a

- fleshly mind (Colossians 2:18)
- vain mind (Ephesians 4:17)
- carnal mind (Romans 8:7)
- reprobate mind (Romans 1:28)
- and a doubtful mind (Luke 12:29)

In order for the head to work effectively in the Body of Christ, we must "renew" our minds, as Paul admonishes us to do in Romans chapter 12. But we must also follow what the Lord says in Mark 12:30,

> *"And thou shalt love the Lord thy God with all thy heart, and with all thy soul, and with all thy mind, and with all thy strength: this is the first commandment."*

When we love the Lord God with all our mind, we then receive the mind of Christ.

> 1 Corinthians 2:16, *"For who hath known the mind of the Lord, that he may instruct him? But we have the mind of Christ."*

The mind of Christ is a

- ready mind (Acts 17:11)
- humble mind (Acts 20:19)
- united mind (1 Corinthians 1:10)
- fervent mind (2 Corinthians 7:7)
- willing mind (2 Corinthians 8:12)
- sound mind (2 Timothy 1:7)
- And a mind of wisdom (Revelation 17:9).

Psalms 115 describes many churches and denominations that we see today. It says, *"they have mouths, but they speak not: eyes have they, but they see not: they have ears, but they hear not: noses have they but they smell not."* The apostolic anointing is an anointing that thinks the thoughts of God, hears the voice of God, sees the vision of God, speaks the word of God and discerns the spirits in the congregation. If the church leaders want the church to grow, they MUST find the apostolic anointing and allow the people with those gifts to function IN those gifts in order for the Body to perform the call of God with excellence.

Psalms 115 goes on to tell us how to become the Body that thinks, hears, sees, speaks and discerns the will of God. The Psalmist admonishes us to trust God (verses 9 and 10), and fear the Lord (verse 11). Those who trust and fear the Lord will be blessed by Him!

3
~The Shoulders~

The shoulder joint is a complex arrangement of bones, muscles, ligaments and tendons. The shoulders facilitate movements of the arm. Shoulders are also used as a platform to sit transport heavy items. According to healthpages.org, the shoulder is very versatile, allowing the arm to execute fine motor skills, such as picking up small items, as well as gross motor skills, such as throwing and lifting.

Shoulders, in the Spirit realm, represent the prophets. Prophesy in the original Greek text means "to speak forth by divine inspirations, to predict, to utter forth, declare a thing which can only be known by divine revelation; to break forth under sudden impulse in lofty discourse or praise of the divine counsels." Basically, the prophet conveys the voice of the Lord.

Temple Building: Realigning The Body of Christ

Prophets in the Old Testament were respected by all…most of the time. Prophets governed the religious order in Bible days. They were invited to bless government leaders when a change of leadership took place, after all, to receive a blessing from a prophet was like receiving a blessing from God himself. Kings even appointed personal prophets to guide them in governing the country.

Prophets went by many names. A prophet could be called a seer, Man of God, or a visionary. When God spoke, the prophet heard. And, when the prophet heard, he or she relayed that word to the people.

So, you may be asking what this has to do with the shoulders.

"For unto us a child is born, unto us a son is given: and the government shall be upon his shoulder…" Isaiah 9:6.

The church is the body of the Son! The government rests on his shoulders. A government is a group of individuals chosen to exercise authoritative direction for the whole body. In the Bible kings and commoners alike consulted the prophets to receive "authoritative direction" for some phase of their lives. The prophet would then consult God and relay that message to the people.

When God gave Moses the design for the Tabernacle, the place where God communed with the people, each furnishing had a special spiritual meaning. The Ark of the Covenant, also called the Ark or God or the Ark of Testimony, was the furnishing that housed the Book of the Law, Aaron's rod that budded and Manna from heaven. The Book of the Law is the Ten Commandments. It was the

~The Shoulders~

ultimate symbol of government and order. Aaron's rod that budded was the symbol of authority to show that only God may call a person to serve in his presence. And the Manna from heaven represented God's daily provision. The Ark was shielded from the public by a veil, which only the High Priest could enter. The people were edified, exhorted and comforted by the priests who consulted God on their behalf at the Ark.

The Ark was the place where God's presence dwelled as a cloud by day and a pillar of fire by night. The High Priest consulted God at the Ark of the Covenant in order to govern the people and find out the next MOVE the people were to make. There were special Levites appointed to carry the Ark of the Covenant when the people were on the move to another area. These Levites would insert polls into rings on the bottom of the Ark and carry it on their shoulders. The appointed Levites carried the presence of God and the order, authority and provision of God on their shoulders. (Exodus 25, 28, 37).

> *"Then David said, 'None ought to carry the ark of God but the Levites: for them hath the LORD chosen to carry the ark of God, and to minister unto him forever.' And the children of the Levites bare the ark of God upon their shoulders with the staves thereon, as Moses commanded according to the word of the Lord,"* 1 Chronicles 15:2, 15 (KJV).

The three contents of the Ark of the Covenant relate to the three characteristics of a prophetic word.

Temple Building: Realigning The Body of Christ

"But he that prophesieth speaketh unto men to edification, and exhortation, and comfort," I Corinthians 14:3 (KJV).

Prophets hear, or envision, a word of God and relay that message to his people for their edification. Edification in the original Greek means "to build up; the act of one who promotes another's growth in Christian wisdom, piety, happiness, holiness." Edification is defined in merriam-webster.com as to "teach someone in a way that improves their mind or character." The Manna that was placed in the Ark of the Covenant was a reminder that God will always provide what is needed to edify (build up and improve) His people.

Prophets hear, or envision, a word of God and relay that message to his people for their exhortation. Exhortation can also be interpreted as encouragement. Merriam-Webster defines exhortation as trying to "influence someone by words or advice." The prophet's words impart a level of authority into the hearer. Aaron's rod budded because God wanted to show the people that He had given Aaron (a descendant of Levi) authority to serve as High Priest (Numbers 17). That authority followed Aaron's bloodline until Jesus' death, when the veil to the Ark was torn in two, giving everyone individual access to the presence of God at the Ark (Mark 15:38; Luke 23:45; Matthew 27:51; 2 Corinthians 3:17-18). A prophetic word of exhortation gives the receiver authority to go boldly before God to accomplish the calling on his or her life.

Prophets hear, or envision, a word from God and relay that message to his people for their comfort. In merriam-webster.com, comfort means "to cause someone to feel less worried, upset, frightened; to give strength and hope." Psalm 119:52 (NIV) says, "I remember, LORD, your ancient laws, and I find comfort in them." The Book of the Law was placed in the Ark of the Covenant to remind us that God's order, found in scripture, should cause us to "feel less worried, upset and frightened," and give us renewed "strength and hope."

The promises of edification (manna), exhortation (authority), and comfort (law) rest on the shoulders of the prophets.

Isaiah 22:22 says, *"And the key of the house of David will I lay upon his SHOULDER; so he shall open, and none shall shut; and he shall shut, and none shall open."* The key is inserted into the key hole and turned by the collective work of the arms and hands. These are the other gifts that come out of the prophetic gifting, which is represented by the shoulders.

The Arms

The arms come out of the shoulders and they work with the hands for lifting, carrying, pushing and pulling things. The arm consists of five sections the upper arm, elbow, forearm, wrist and hand. Likewise, there are five spiritual gifts that come out of the prophetic gifting. They are words of knowledge, words of wisdom, intercession, impartation and healing/deliverance.

The upper arm

The upper arm provides strength in the area of pulling and lifting. The upper arm represents words of knowledge. A word of knowledge is knowing something about someone that you would not know if someone had not told you. Someone with this gift is allowing the Holy Spirit to transmit his knowledge, which is knowledge of EVERYTHING, into their mind's eye.

"Apply thine heart unto instruction, and thine ears to the words of knowledge," Proverbs 23:12.

For example, I met a woman at a dance conference and the Holy Spirit showed me her house and he showed me children around her at her house. As I told her about her house, she began to scream, and she confirmed that she had an in home daycare. She had been at a crossroads in her line of work and that word of knowledge confirmed to her that she needed to continue to run her in home daycare.

As we discussed earlier, knowledge is information. A word of knowledge is information, given by the Holy Spirit, to allow the hearer to know that God has heard their prayers and the answer is on the way. Words of knowledge pull people into their destined direction and lift them to a higher level of spirituality.

The forearm

The forearm is the area between the wrist and the elbow. According to healthline.com, the forearm allows the arm to rotate and twist. Spiritually, the forearm represents words of wisdom. Sometimes a word of knowledge is not enough to help a person solve their own problem. That's where words of wisdom come in.

"For to one is given by the Spirit the word of wisdom; to another the word of knowledge by the same Spirit," I Corinthians 12:8 (KJV).

Words of wisdom rotate the word of knowledge into an exact instruction for the hearer. In the same conversation with the woman in the above example, the Holy Spirit gave me a word of wisdom for her. She had hurt her foot during the conference, which was another sign of the direction God was leading her. The Holy Spirit told me, and I shared with her, that if she continued to dance the same thing that happened to her left foot would happen to the right. She knew exactly what that meant. She had been praying about her place in the dance ministry. God was telling her through this word of wisdom that her place was a more administrative role, not physically dancing.

The word of wisdom is a word of direct application to a person's life. A word of wisdom can come after a word of knowledge, or it can stand alone. It can be a long, drawn out command or it can be one word. In either case, the word of wisdom tells the hearer what God desires for them.

The elbow

The elbow is a hinge joint that connects the upper arm and the forearm. It allows the arm to bend and extend to 180 degrees. The elbow allows the arm to move in such a way that makes lifting, carrying, pushing and pulling possible.

Temple Building: Realigning The Body of Christ

I believe the elbow represents the intercessors of the Body. An intercessor is the prayer warrior of the church. Intercessors received a burden from God to pray on behalf of a person, community or circumstance.

"But if they be prophets, and if the word of the Lord be with them, let them now make intercession to the Lord of hosts, that the vessels which are left in the house of the Lord, and the house of the king of Judah, and at Jerusalem go not to Babylon," Jeramiah 27:18 (KJV).

Intercession in the original Hebrew text is paga`, Strong's Concordance number 293. In addition to "intercession," the word also means to encounter, reach, and meet. The elbow MEETS with the forearm and the upper arm so the arm can extend to 180 degrees, making it easier for the body to REACH for things the body needs! Likewise, the intercessor MEETS with God and connects His will with the need to be met, so the body can REACH its purpose!

James Goll says about prophetic intercessors in his book *The Seer: The Prophetic Power of Visions, Dreams and Open Heavens*, they don't just pray to God, but they "pray the prayers of God." An intercessor will constantly pray and fast for the answered prayer.

Nehemiah was an intercessor: *"And it came to pass, when I heard these words, that I sat down and wept, and mourned certain days, and fasted, and prayed before the God of heaven," Nehemiah 1:4.* Nehemiah MEET with God to help Jerusalem REACH the goal of rebuilding the city's walls.

Anna was an intercessor: *"And there was one Anna, a prophetess, the daughter of Phanuel, of the tribe of Aser: she was of a great age, and had lived with an husband seven years from her*

~The Shoulders~

virginity; *³⁷And she was a widow of about fourscore and four years, which departed not from the temple, but served God with fastings and prayers night and day," Luke 2:36-37*. Anna MEET with God to REACH her goal of seeing the Messiah before she died.

Jesus is an intercessor: *"Who is he that condemneth? It is Christ that died, yea rather, that is risen again, who is even at the right hand of God, who also maketh intercession for us," Romans 8:34*. Jesus continually MEETS with God to REACH the goal of His Body going forth in excellence!

The intercessors of the church may spend hours praying. They will "pray without ceasing" as Paul says in I Thessalonians 5:17, until that prayer is answered or until the burning desire to pray for that particular issue is alleviated. The church should allow parishioners with this special gift to exercise that gift because "the effectual fervent prayer of a righteous man availeth much," James 5:16b.

The wrist and hand

"Thus saith the LORD of hosts; Let your hands be strong, ye that hear in these days these words by the mouth of the prophets, which were in the day that the foundation of the house of the LORD of hosts was laid, that the temple might be built," Zechariah 8:9 (KJV).

I am going to put the wrist and the hand together because the wrist is part of the hand and you cannot operate one without the other. The hand is the most versatile and useful tool in all of creation. There are parts of the hand, the fingers, the palm, the back hand and the wrist.

Temple Building: Realigning The Body of Christ

The wrist connects the arm with the hand. It is this network of bones that gives the hand the ability to move around for fine motor tasks like picking up small items, and stabilize for gross motor tasks such as pushing and pulling. The back of the hand is an object of great force when balled into a fist. It can be used somewhat like a hammer when operated properly. The palm is also a very strong part of the hand also used for hitting and holding. The fingers are the last part of the hand. They distinguish humans from any other species of life. The fingers make it possible for the hands to grasp and hold objects of various sizes and shapes.

In the Bible, the hand has several functions. The arms and hands were lifted in worship. They were also lifted in war. The arms and hands were used in judgment. And then there was the "laying on of hands." The laying on of hands is used to seize someone or discipline them. The laying on of hands is also used to commission new leadership as well as for impartation, healing and deliverance.

Commissioning-

Commissioning is the act of giving authority. When the servants of the Lord in the following scriptures were being elevated to another level in the ministry, the leader laid hands on them. The process of laying hands during a commissioning signaled to the congregation that the leader approved of the one being commissioned and if the congregation held the old leader in high esteem, they should hold the new leader in high esteem as well.

~The Shoulders~

"While they were worshiping the Lord and fasting, the Holy Spirit said, "Set apart for me Barnabas and Saul for the work to which I have called them." ³So after they had fasted and prayed, they placed their hands on them and sent them off," Acts 13:1-3.

"This proposal pleased the whole group. They chose Stephen, a man full of faith and of the Holy Spirit; also Philip, Procorus, Nicanor, Timon, Parmenas, and Nicolas from Antioch, a convert to Judaism. They presented these men to the apostles, who prayed and laid their hands on them," Acts 6:5-6.

"Now Joshua son of Nun was filled with the spirit of wisdom because Moses had laid his hands on him. So the Israelites listened to him and did what the Lord had commanded Moses," Deuteronomy 34:9.

<u>Healing-</u>

Sometimes, when I don't feel well, all I need is a hug and I'm all better! Touching someone releases a spiritual connection to that person. If you touch them in anger they will experience fear and anger. If you touch them in love, they will experience love and rejuvenation. When Jesus touched the individuals that he healed, a portion of His spirit was transferred to them. Jesus' spirit is undefiled and His body cannot be tainted by sickness, infirmity, or disease. When we, the body of Christ, institute a ministry of healing through touch, we must have a pure mind and clean heart. We must touch with the intention of transferring Jesus' pure and

Temple Building: Realigning The Body of Christ

undefiled Spirit of love to the individual, and by faith that person will be healed.

> *"At sunset, the people brought to Jesus all who had various kinds of sickness, and laying his hands on each one, he healed them,"* Luke 4:40.

> *"They shall take up serpents; and if they drink any deadly thing, it shall not hurt them; they shall lay hands on the sick, and they shall recover,"* Mark 16:18.

> *"His father was sick in bed, suffering from fever and dysentery. Paul went in to see him and, after prayer, placed his hands on him and healed him,"* Acts 28:8 (NIV).

Impartation-

Whatever is in you, you have the power to impart that to other through the laying on of hands. Paul discusses the Spiritual Gifts in the books of Corinthians, Romans and Galatians. Jesus said that he would send the Holy Spirit. Now, those who have received the Holy Spirit should freely give that Spirit of power to others.

> *"Neglect not the gift that is in thee, which was given thee by prophecy, with the laying on of the hands of the presbytery,"* I Timothy 4:14.

> *"Then laid they their hands on them, and they received the Holy Ghost,"* Acts 8:17.

There is so much power in the hands! As I said earlier, some churches have completely disabled the shoulders arms and hands, thus cutting off the gifts that are connected to the

~The Shoulders~

prophetic office and gifting. If a limb is not used it develops atrophy, which means it withers and becomes less effective.

People with a prophetic gift in a traditional, religious church are conditioned to suppress that gift. As one of these prophetic people in a traditional church, I was told my prophetic dreams "could be considered evil." My request to intercede on behalf of an incarcerated member was ignored. If I laid my hands on someone, I might as well had given them an incurable disease! The Lord told Moses that priests with certain bodily deformities could not minister before Him in the Tabernacle.

> *[16] The Lord said to Moses, [17] "Say to Aaron: 'For the generations to come none of your descendants who has a defect may come near to offer the food of his God. [18] No man who has any defect may come near: no man who is blind or lame, disfigured or deformed;* <u>*[19] no man with a crippled foot or hand*</u>*…[22] He may eat the most holy food of his God, as well as the holy food; 23yet because of his defect, he must not go near the curtain or approach the altar, and so desecrate my sanctuary. I am the Lord, who makes them holy,' "* (Leviticus 21:16-19, 22-23- NIV).

But, Jesus can heal lame hands and arms!

> *"[1] Another time Jesus went into the synagogue, and a man with a shriveled hand was there. [2] Some of them were looking for a reason to accuse Jesus, so they watched him closely to see if he would heal him on the*

Temple Building: Realigning The Body of Christ

Sabbath. ³Jesus said to the man with the shriveled hand, "Stand up in front of everyone." ⁴Then Jesus asked them, 'Which is lawful on the Sabbath: to do good or to do evil, to save life or to kill?" But they remained silent. ⁵He looked around at them in anger and, deeply distressed at their stubborn hearts, said to the man, "Stretch out your hand.' He stretched it out, and his hand was completely restored," Mark 3:1-5 (NIV).

Jesus was upset that the church was too stubborn to accept the gift of healing! Is Jesus happy with His body having "shriveled arms" today?!

All it took was for this man to MOVE the hand in FAITH for the hand to be healed! When churches begin to exercise the gifts already in the body, the atrophy will be reversed and the body will begin to be restored! Once the body regains the use of its limbs, then it can move into its calling again.

4
~The Hips~

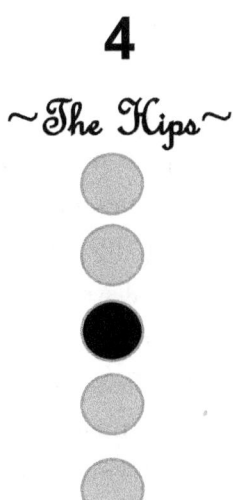

The hips, according to innerbody.com, are one of the most flexible joints in the body. The ball and socket joints of the hips are the second most flexible joints in the body behind the shoulder joints. They allow 360° movement of the leg, which allows inward (pigeon toed) as well as outward rotation, a concept dancers appropriately call turn-out.

There are four basic movements of the hips:

1. Flexion- The hip joint bends to allow the body to achieve lower levels of movement such as sitting, bending down, etc.
2. Extension- The hip joint straightens to allow the body to achieve upper levels of movement such as standing and jumping.
3. Abduction- The hip joint allows the leg to be lifted away from the body, like in a kick.

4. Adduction- The hip joint allows the leg to be brought back into the body.

The bones that make up the pelvis/hip area act as a connection between the upper half of the body and the lower half of the body. These bones create a well to house and protect the lower organs of the digestive system, the reproductive system and renal system,

The reproductive system allows the human body, when joined with a body of the opposite sex, to reproduce another human body. The male reproductive organs sow seeds and the female reproductive organs receive seeds, grow them and bear the result of that growth, another human being. For this reason, the pelvic are represents the Evangelist.

Merriam-webster.com defines and evangelist as "a person and especially a preacher who tries to convince people to become Christian." The Strong's Concordance defines an evangelist as "a bringer of good tidings." Both definitions confirm that the evangelist should be the "reproductive system" of the Body of Christ.

2 Timothy 4:5 (KJV),

"But watch thou in all things, endure afflictions, do the work of an evangelist, make proof of thy ministry."

The role of the evangelist is to produce "proof" or fruit of the ministry. Evangelism is a God-given gift to preach the Gospel of Salvation to unbelievers effectively, so that their response is to believe in Jesus and become a part of the body of Christ.

~The Hips~

Effective evangelism can be seen in the story of Philip, the deacon and evangelist spoken of in the book of Acts. The name Philip means "lover of horses." Horses are known for traveling long distances with great speed. Evangelists too, are travelers by nature. Acts 8:4 says, *"Those who had been scattered preached the word wherever they went."* They find great pleasure in spreading the gospel to different communities and people groups. Philip, in Acts chapter 8, is seen preaching the Gospel of Jesus in three different cities. In each city, the people listened to his preaching, were blessed by the signs and wonders he performed, were baptized with water and Spirit, and became followers of Jesus Christ.

In Acts chapter 6, Philip is chosen as one of the original seven deacons of the church. The criteria for becoming a deacon was to be full of the Holy Spirit and wisdom. The deacons' responsibility was to take care of "feeding" the people of the church. Evangelists love "feeding" or "sowing into" people literally, that is taking care of their needs, and spiritually with the word of God.

The renal system consists of the kidneys, ureter, bladder and urethra. The renal system works with the respiratory, integumentary (skin), circulatory, and digestive systems is to filter the blood of waste and flush it out of the body. Blood enters the kidneys to be cleaned out and pumped back through the body. The waste that was removed from the blood then leaves the kidneys through the ureter and is stored in the bladder. When the bladder is full it signals the urethra to open and allow the waste to exit the body.

Temple Building: Realigning The Body of Christ

The renal system is a picture of the gift of discernment of demonic spirits. This may sound a little scary if you have never encountered a demonic spirit before, but you will become more at ease by the end of this chapter!

Demonic spirits are as real as angelic ones. Ephesians 6:12 essentially says that we make think we are having conflict with people, but in actuality, we are "wrestling" demonic influences. Verses 13-14 continues to command us to put on the armor of God. The "belt of truth" protects the hip/evangelistic area from demonic influences.

At the time this passage of scripture was written, the belt of the Roman soldier was one of the most important pieces of the armor. It not only held the rest of the garment in place, it was also used to sheath the sword, and the stripes of leather that hung from the belt provided protection of the lower part of the body.

Paul is telling us in Ephesians 6 that the Gospel Truth about Jesus protects the body and functions as the place to hold the "Sword of the Spirit, which is the word of God." First Thessalonians 5:21 says, "Test all things; <u>hold fast</u> what is good." The word of God is good! The word of God is our weapon of warfare and the belt of truth is its resting place. That belt is firmly placed around the waist of the soldier because the Evangelist is responsible for spreading that Word of Truth.

> Hebrews 4:12, *"For the word of God is quick and powerful, and shaper than any two-edged sword, piercing even to the dividing asunder of soul and spirit,*

~The Hips~

and joints and marrow and is a discerner of the thoughts and intents of the heart."

The renal system discerns the nutrients in the blood from the waste and expels the waste from the body. Evangelists are called to minister in various places in the world. They will need to discern if the place where he will go to minister is ready for the truth or inundated with demonic influences that he will have to war against.

In John 17:17, Jesus asks God to "Sanctify them through thy truth: thy word is truth."

The hips can be the most powerful part of the body. The pelvic area can be an agent of good or evil! If moved in a certain way, the hips can cause a person to think bad thoughts! The biblical example I think of most is Salome, Herod's step-daughter and niece, whose dance pleased Herod so much he promised her anything she wanted up to half the kingdom. At the urging of her mother, Salome asked for John the Baptist's head.

I'm willing to bet that dance wasn't a praise dance! Every television and movie depiction of this biblical event has her provocatively moving her hips, silently seducing Herod into her spell. Does that sound familiar? Much of the popular dances today emulate movements of intercourse. Popular songs and dances of today encourage the listener to think about having sexual relations, often with someone the hearer is not married to. The spirit of sexual immorality is the biggest enemy to the evangelistic anointing.

Temple Building: Realigning The Body of Christ

1 Corinthians 6:13, 18-20 NIV

> *You say, "Food for the stomach and the stomach for food, and God will destroy them both." The body, however, is not meant for sexual immorality but for the Lord, and the Lord for the body. Flee from sexual immorality. All other sins a person commits are outside the body, but whoever sins sexually, sins against their own body. Do you not know that your bodies are temples of the Holy Spirit, who is in you, whom you have received from God? You are not your own; you were bought at a price. Therefore honor God with your bodies.*

Paul is writing to the Corinthians, a nation known for sexual immorality as a form of worship to their pagan gods. It was such a common practice that they felt that it was accepted in this new Christian way. However, Paul tells the Corinthians that sexual immorality is a sin against the individual body as well as the body of Christ.

Many churches ignore the topic of sex. Teaching on the appropriate purpose and activity of sexual intercourse and reproduction will help strengthen the evangelistic gifting in the body. The story of Noah and the Ark is a story of restoration of appropriate sexual activity in the body. God was so upset about the sexual impurity that had become so common place on the earth, that he commanded Noah to build the ark and place his family, along with a male and a female representative of each animal on the earth in it.

~The Hips~

When Noah, his family and all the animals came out of the ark, God commanded them to "be fruitful and multiply," Genesis 8:15-17.

This is the ultimate evangelistic mandate. This mandate is still applicable to the body of Christ today. Galatians 6: 7-8 speaks to this mandate. It says,

> *"Be not deceived; God is not mocked: for whatsoever a man soweth, that shall he also reap. For he that soweth to his flesh shall of the flesh reap corruption; but he that soweth to the Spirit shall of the Spirit reap life everlasting."*

The evangelist sows seeds. And, when those seeds are nurtured, they produce fruit. But, the body must be careful about the type of seeds that it is sowing.

> *"The acts of the flesh are obvious: sexual immorality, impurity and debauchery* (which is bad or immoral behavior involving sex, drugs or alcohol); *idolatry and witchcraft; hatred, discord, jealousy, fits of rage, selfish ambition, dissensions, factions and envy; drunkenness, orgies, and the like. I warn you, as I did before, that those who live like this will not inherit the kingdom of God,"* Galatians 5:19-21 (NIV).

If any of the seeds mention above are sown into the body, the body will produce the fruit of that behavior! If you find your body producing that fruit, you may need to check the seed that have been sown, not just in that particular body, but also check the bloodline of that body. Only repentance and testimony and the blood of Jesus can kill the seeds of the flesh.

Revelation 12:11 (KJV),
> *"And they overcame him by the blood of the Lamb, and by the word of their testimony; and they loved not their lives unto the death."*

Galatians 5:22-24 tells us the fruit that the body bears when the Spirit sows the seed:
> *"But the fruit of the Spirit is love, joy, peace, forbearance, kindness, goodness, faithfulness, gentleness, and self-control. Against such things there is no law. Those who belong to Christ Jesus have crucified the flesh with its passions and desires."*

These are the seeds the evangelist of Jesus should sow! When these seeds are sown, the body of Christ becomes "fruitful and multiplies."

5
~The Knees~

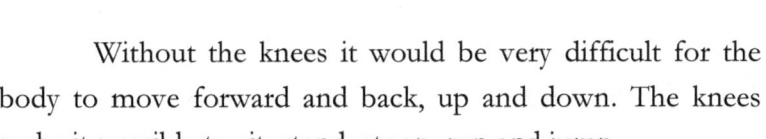

Without the knees it would be very difficult for the body to move forward and back, up and down. The knees make it possible to sit, stand, stoop, run and jump.

The knee is a hinge joint made of bones, ligaments, cartilage, and tendons that, when working with the feet and hips, makes loco-motor movement possible. As the hinge opens, it LEADS the foot extend to extend forward. When the foot is planted on the ground, it provides a foundation that allows the weight of the body to be propelled forward with precision, strength and stability, thus creating forward movement!

We've all heard the phrase "lift with your knees and not with your back." The knees were especially created to carry the weight for the body. The cartilage in the knees acts as a shock absorber for the body. When the body carries too much weight for an extended period of time, the cartilage wears out, causing the knees to weaken. The bones rubbing together cause pain in the knee joints even when the body is performing very menial tasks. Even a small amount of weight loss takes a tremendous amount of pressure off the knees.

The knees of the physical body represent the pastors of the Body of Christ. Just as the knees allow the body to move forward, aid in lifting and carrying things to a higher level and/or a different place, and provide strength and stability, the pastor leads the church in movement, carries the emotional weight of the church, and feeds them knowledge and understanding to live a righteous life.

According to merriam-webster.com, "pastor" is a "spiritual overseer." The word is derived from the Latin word meaning "herdsman." The Bible often uses the analogy of the shepherd to explain the pastor's role in the church.

Pastors are to care for the people of the church as a shepherd cares for the sheep. They are to be leaders of the congregation, as Moses prays in Numbers 27:15-17,

> *"And Moses spake unto the Lord, saying, Let the Lord, the God of the spirits of all flesh, set a man over the congregation, which may go out before them, and which may go in before them, and which may lead them out, and which may bring them in; that the congregation of the Lord be not as sheep which have no shepherd."*

~The Knees~

The shepherd/pastor should be a leader for the congregation. As a hinge joint of the knee, the pastor should lead by example and be OPENLY share their testimony, as Revelation 12:10 says that our testimony helps "us" overcome. The pastor cares for the flock so much so, that he/she will do anything to lead them forward. Anything includes "bringing them in" or correct unrighteous behavior. It is the pastor's responsibility to confront ungodly actions reactions that are happening within the church IN LOVE, with the intention to lift the congregants, not bring them down.

Just like the knees, the pastors of the church carry the weight of the Body. Isaiah 40:11 says, "He shall feed his flock like a shepherd: he shall gather the lambs with his arm and carry them in his bosom, and shall gently lead those that are with young." When I read this scripture I think of the painting I would see on church fans when I was younger, of Jesus carrying a lamb on his shoulders. Pastors should embody that portrait of Jesus. Pastors are responsible for showing the church how to be in the world but not of the world. As Christians, we are to handle the situations we go through in life with dignity and grace. The pastor should nurture, care for, and guide people toward on-going spiritual maturity (lifting up) and becoming more like Christ.

Pastors should also develop strength and stability within the Body of Christ through "feeding" them the word of God. I Peter 5:1-4 (KJV) says,

"The elders which are among you I exhort, who am also an elder, and a witness of the sufferings of Christ, and also a

Temple Building: Realigning The Body of Christ

partaker of the glory that shall be revealed: Feed the flock of God which is among you, taking the oversight thereof, not by constraint, but willingly; not for filthy lucre, but of a ready mind; Neither as being lords over God's heritage, but being ensamples to the flock. And when the chief Shepherd shall appear, ye shall receive a crown of glory that fadeth not away."

According to this scripture, the pastor should be willing to "feed" the people through the word of God. Jeremiah 3:15 says the pastor should feed the flock with knowledge and understanding. This Spiritual food should nourish the body to make it strong, much like the knees give strength to the body. Peter further explains that the pastor should be an example to the rest of the church and help the body function in excellence, as he/she functions in excellence.

As I said before, the knees begin to break down when they are responsible for carrying too much weight. It is the same for the pastors in our local bodies. Too often, the pastor is acting in the role of all the 5-fold ministries and he/she is often worn out by the work he/she is called upon to do. Unfortunately, we are all too willing to allow the pastor to do all this work, and he/she is all too willing to do it!

The Bible tells us how to lose some of that weight that is burdening our pastors… exercise!

I Timothy 4:8 (NIV), *"For physical training is of some value, but godliness has value for all things, holding promise for both the present life and the life to come."*

~The Knees~

We will discuss exercise in a later chapter, but, for now, let's look at common injuries to the knees and how those injuries can be healed spiritually.

The knee is the largest joint in the body. Because it is such an important joint, it is very susceptible to injury. The most common injuries to the knees include fractures, sprains and ligament tears, and dislocations. These injuries cause instability of the knee, which effects the whole body.

Pastors, like the knee, can become fractured, sprained and torn. As a pastor, you are called on to provide emotional support, counseling, preaching and prayer. But, in all that providing, who is providing for the pastor?! If the body is aligned properly, the pastor will be edified by the Apostle, Prophet and Evangelist of the body, and vice versa. The leadership team is given to not only edify the body, but to encourage each other as well.

Pastors, like the knee, can become dislocated. Dislocation occurs when the bones of the joint are out of place. This injury can happen in any joint, but most commonly happens in the knees, fingers, hips and shoulders. Leaders can begin to act on their own, forgetting the will of God, when pride sets in. Members can begin to act on their own when they feel their gifts are not being utilized or appreciated in a particular body. This is dislocation.

Dislocation occurred in Exodus 32 when the children of Israel convinced Aaron to make a god for them to worship, forgetting the God who brought them out of slavery. Dislocation occurred in I Samuel 13 when King Saul decided to dedicate offering to God without the prophet

Samuel being present. Dislocation occurred in Matthew 26 when Judas agreed to betray Jesus.

The answer to preventing dislocation can be found in Isaiah 40:31, *"But they that wait upon the Lord shall renew their strength; they shall mount up with wings as eagles; they shall run, and not be weary; and they shall walk, and not faint."*

We must "wait" on the Lord. The Hebrew word for "wait" means "to expect." We must "wait" on the Lord, and "expect" him to move us in the direction we are to move. Moving the body on your own will ALWAYS cause problems in one way or another.

> *"Trust in the Lord with all thine heart; and lean not unto thine own understanding. In all thy ways acknowledge him, and he shall direct thy paths. Be not wise in thine own eyes: fear the Lord and depart from evil. It shall be health to thy navel, and marrow to the bones."*
> Proverbs 3:5-8 (KJV).

The Hebrew word for wait" also means to be wound together for strength, as a rope. The decision maker(s) of your body must be wound together with God, and each other, in order to become strong enough to move the body, without becoming tired!

Avoid injury to the knee by becoming re-aligned today!

6

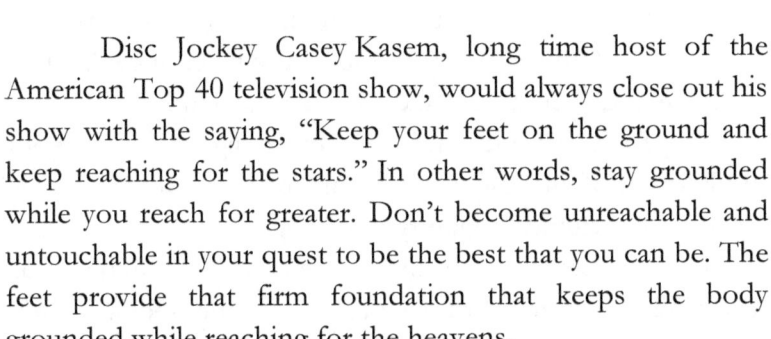

Disc Jockey Casey Kasem, long time host of the American Top 40 television show, would always close out his show with the saying, "Keep your feet on the ground and keep reaching for the stars." In other words, stay grounded while you reach for greater. Don't become unreachable and untouchable in your quest to be the best that you can be. The feet provide that firm foundation that keeps the body grounded while reaching for the heavens.

The foot is comprised of a series of bones, muscles and joints at the end of the leg that balances weight and facilitates locomotor movements. Locomotor movements take the body places. In other words, the feet are not needed if the body does not move.

Feet have 3 sections; the hind foot, the midfoot and the forefoot.

The hind foot is made up of the ankle joint and the heel joint. The ankle joint and heel joint work together to provide stability for the body. The ankle joint is very flexible, allowing the foot to move in all 4 directions, up, down, left and right, as well as in a circular motion. This flexibility of movement allows the foot to adjust quickly to changes in balance that the body must make when moving quickly. The hind foot connects the foot to the leg, which is also instrumental in the locomotor movements of the body.

The midfoot is comprised of the arches of the foot, which is a shock absorber when the body lands out of a jump or in the lifting and/or carrying more weight.

The forefoot includes the ball of the foot and the toes. The forefoot works similarly to the hand in that it grasps and grips to give the body flexibility when ascending and descending difficult terrain.

Without feet, the body could not move itself. Without feet, the body does not have the ability to balance. Without feet, the body could not handle unstable ground.

If the feet and knees are not in alignment, the whole body is out of alignment. Misalignment of the feet and knees creates opportunity for injury of the legs.

The feet represent the teachers of the church because the teachers create a firm foundation for the body of Christ, much like the feet for the physical body. Teachers are responsible for communicating biblical principles and sound doctrine to the people of the church so they apply those truths in their daily lives. They help the body turn knowledge into understanding and understanding into a Christian walk with wisdom. So, in essence, the teacher helps the congregants "walk it out."

When the Bible talks about feet, it often references the step, the walk and the path, also called the way. Teachers help the body take steps that leads to an excellent walk on the straight and narrow path.

"For we WALK by faith and not by sight," 2 Corinthians 5:7 (KJV).

³Jesus knew that the Father had put all things under his power, and that he had come from God and was returning to God; ⁴so he got up from the meal, took off his outer clothing, and wrapped a towel around his waist. ⁵After that, he poured water into a basin and began to wash his disciples' **feet***, drying them with the towel that was wrapped around him. Jesus answered, "Unless I wash you, you have no part with me." ⁹"Then, Lord," Simon Peter replied, "not just my feet but my hands and my head as well!" ¹⁰Jesus answered, "<u>Those who have had a bath need only to wash their</u>* **feet***<u>; their whole body is clean</u>. And you are clean, though not every one of you." "Do you understand what I have done for you?" he asked them. ¹³"<u>You call me</u>* **'Teacher'** *<u>and 'Lord,' and rightly so, for that is what I am</u>.* **¹⁴Now that I, your Lord and Teacher, have washed your feet, you also should wash one another's feet.** (John 13:3-5, 9-10, 13-14; NIV)

Of all the scriptures confirming the feet as the representation of the teacher, this is the one I love the most! Jesus, The Teacher, tells us that as teachers in His likeness, we should wash each other's feet! Do you think He meant to literally go around washing people's feet? No! Jesus is teaching His disciples to be teachers. How do you figuratively wash someone's feet? You make sure that the teaching they are receiving is clean, pure and undefiled. Make sure the teaching keeps the people in step with God, walking forward and not backward, and moving on the straight and narrow path!

Remember what Jesus told His disciples to do when they encountered a town that would not accept His teaching; He told them to shake the dust off their feet (Matthew 10:14; Mark 6:11; Luke 9:5). It was ancient Jewish custom to shake the dust off your feet as a sign that the territory was unclean. Jesus is commanding the disciples to keep their teaching clean from worldly influences that may take them off the course on which He set them. As Jesus' disciples, we must learn from this example of holiness. Churches, and teachers in the church, often feel that they must teach a lesson that is pleasing to the people. That thought process is dusty! Teachers should teach the people how to live in practical holiness; that is to be IN the world but not OF the world!

Each foot has five toes, ten toes in all. Ten is the number of divine order. Teachers should order the word that has been preached and prophesied so that the body can deal with adverse situations and terrains that happen on a daily basis.

> *"Order my steps in thy word: and let not any iniquity have dominion over me," Psalms 119:133 (KJV).*
> *"The steps of a good man are ordered by the Lord: and he delighteth in his way," Psalms 37:23 (KJV).*

God desires to order each step we make with righteousness and goodness. Each toe represents a different subject that teachers should teach to bring order into the body.

~The Foot~

1. <u>Teachers should teach fear of the Lord</u>. Psalms 34:11 says, *"Come ye children, hearken unto me: I will teach you the fear of the Lord."* Fear hear means to reverence God and hold him in high respect. When we hold someone in such high esteem that we "fear" we will do whatever He asks.

2. <u>Teachers should teach the word of God</u>. Acts 18:11 says, *"And he continued there a year and six months, teaching the word of God among them."* The foundation of the body must be in the undefiled Word of God. We must teach this word to the members of the body so they know God's will for each member individually and collectively.

3. <u>Teachers should teach God's ordinances and laws</u>. Exodus 18:20 says, *"And thou shalt teach them ordinances and laws, and shalt shew them the way wherein they must walk, and the work that they must do."* In addition to the Word of God, the body should know his laws. Yes, Jesus redeemed us from the penalty of the law, but we should still know it. The law was set in place to establish God's order for the body when we come into communion with him. We should still make every effort to follow the law in the freedom of knowing that through Jesus we have been saved from the penalty of that law.

4. <u>Teachers should teach Jesus' commands.</u> Jesus says in Matthew 28:20, *"Teaching them to observe all things whatsoever I have commanded you: and, lo, I am with you always, even unto the end of the world. Amen."* Teachers should study Jesus' teachings and decrees and teach them to His people. When we quote Jesus' commands

and decrees, we reaffirm His presence in our lives until He manifests Himself on the earth again. Living His commands gives us power and authority on earth.

5. <u>Teachers should teach the gospel of the kingdom</u>. Matthew 4:23 says, *"And Jesus went about all Galilee, teaching in their synagogues, and preaching the gospel of the kingdom, and healing all manner of sickness and all manner of disease among the people."* Jesus taught the gospel of the kingdom. We are citizens of the Kingdom of God, and we should act as such! But, how do we know how citizens of the kingdom act if we are never taught?! God says over and over again that we are to be holy and set apart, acting as citizens of the Heavenly Kingdom while we are here on earth. This is a teaching that is essential to a foundation on the path of God.

6. <u>Teachers should teach the people how to discern between clean and unclean</u>. Ezekiel 44:23 says, *"And they shall teach my people the difference between the holy and profane, and cause them to discern between the unclean and clean."* But wait! Isn't the gift of discernment a function of the apostolic and evangelistic offices? Yes, but everybody has a nose and kidneys. That means that everybody has the capacity to discern. Teachers are to teach that gift. If you are a parent, you taught your children how to discern between hot and cold. The same is true for the Children of God. He wants us to know the difference between good and bad, holy and profane, clean and unclean. When we know the difference, then we can learn the next lesson, how to deny the things that are not of God.

7. <u>Teachers should teach the body how to deny worldly lusts</u>. Titus 2:12 says, *"Teaching us that, denying ungodliness and worldly lusts, we should live soberly, righteously, and godly, in this present world."* We are inundated with media that encourages us to give in to our desires. It's hard to live a holy lifestyle, when everything around you is tempting you to do something else. However, when the teacher does his job, you will find that living in holiness it not so hard after all!

8. <u>Teachers should follow the lead of Christ and teach the body how to pray</u>. Luke 11:1 says, *"And it came to pass, that as he was praying in a certain place, when he ceased, one of his disciples said unto him, Lord, teach us to pray, as John also taught his disciples."* Prayer is the main form of communication the body has with its Maker. Prayer is also a weapon of warfare. Jesus said we have the power to bind and loose things in heaven and on earth through our prayers of declaration. When teachers teach the people to pray, they have also taught the people how to have a relationship with God and how to use our Kingdom authority on earth.

9. <u>Teachers should teach the body how to war</u>. Judges 3:2 says, *"Only the generations of the children of Israel might know, to teach them war, at the least such as before knew nothing thereof."* God left some enemies in the land to teach the children how to war. Now, He had already promised to deliver the enemy over to the children of Israel, but he still wanted them to learn how to fight. The enemy is still trying to take our blessings and inheritance today. Father God does not want us to

just lay down and take the punishment the enemy is trying to inflict on us. We have to learn how to fight! Sometimes that fight is with our hands. Sometimes it's with our mouths. Sometimes it's with our praise. Teachers are to teach us which weapon of war we should use for each circumstance in our lives.

10. <u>Teachers should teach the way of the Lord.</u>

Psalm 27:11, *"Teach me thy way, O Lord, and lead me in a plain path."*

Psalm 86:11, *"Teach me thy way, O Lord: I will walk in thy truth."*

In summation, the way of the Lord encompasses each of the previous lessons a teacher should teach. The way of the Lord is the fear of the Lord, which is obedience to the word of the Lord, His law and commands that create order in His Kingdom. This order is the teaches us to discern the profane things of the world, so we can deny that power in our lives, pray and war against it.

Isaiah 52:7 says,

"How beautiful upon the mountains are the feet of him that bringeth good tidings, that publisheth peace; that bringeth good tidings of good, that publisheth salvation; that saith unto Zion, Thy God reigneth!"

The feet of the Body of Christ provide a firm foundation for the Body to stand on, facilitate movement of the Body into its destiny and assists the Body in navigating the tough terrain of life.

~The Foot~

Allow the feet to be the feet and bless the feet on their journey of peace!

7
~Muscles, Ligaments, & Blood~

"From him the whole body, joined and held together by every supporting ligament, grows and builds itself up in love, as each part does its work." Ephesians 4:16 (NIV).

The body is a complex network of bones and muscles, held together by ligaments and tendons that, when used collectively, move the body, grow the body, and allow the body to produce functionality.

"And now these three remain: faith, hope and love. But the greatest of these is love," I Corinthians 13:13, NIV.

I believe faith is represented in the muscles of the body, hope is represented in the ligaments and love is the blood.

Muscles

According to innerbody.com, there are three types of muscles in the body: visceral, which are found inside organs, cardiac, muscles of the heart, and skeletal muscles, the muscle system responsible for movement, posture, joint stability and heat production.

Merriam-webster.com defines faith in three basic ways: "allegiance to duty or person, belief and trust in and loyalty to God," and "something that is believed especially with strong conviction; a system of religious beliefs."

Let's look at the two side by side.

Muscle Type	Faith Definition
Visceral muscles are muscles that make organs, such as the stomach, work.	Allegiance to duty or person.
Cardiac muscles operate the <u>heart</u>, which pumps blood throughout the body.	<u>Belief</u> and trust in and loyalty to God.
Skeletal muscle <u>system</u> facilitate movement, posture (alignment), joint stability and heat production.	Something that is believed especially with strong conviction; a <u>system</u> of religious beliefs.

Visceral muscles have a specific duty for the particular organ for which they work!

Cardiac muscles work the heart. Belief in a particular thing comes from the emotions, which are said to be in the "heart." Romans 10:9 says, *"That if thou shalt confess with thy* *mouth the Lord Jesus, and shalt <u>believe in thine heart</u> that God hath raised him from the dead, thou shalt be saved."* Belief is Faith! When we believe wholeheartedly in something, we act as if though what we believe in is our reality. So, I say again, Belief is Faith! We must have faith in God the Father, God the Son and God the Holy Ghost if we are going to accomplish anything, individually and collectively.

Skeletal muscles, attached to the bones by ligaments, facilitate movement of the body, keep the body in alignment, stabilize the joints that connect body parts, and produce heat that burns off fat that is stored in the body when there is no movement.

When you allow skeletal muscles to MOVE the body through exercise, they begin to produce heat. Body heat burns fat, which is produced when the body stores food and nutrients it does not need. Fat is useless! Too much fat can cause the body to move slowly and inefficiently. So, essentially, fat is a byproduct of not MOVING! Fat in turn makes the body heavy, which puts undo stress on the KNEES!

The Body of Christ NEEDS to move. Its whole function is to GO! Allow the muscles of The Body to perform the duties for which they were created.

Ligaments

Ligaments are long, tough bands of tissue that connect the bones to each other. Their purpose is to give strength and stability to our joints. Healthpages.org describes the ligaments as not being very flexible.

Much like a ligament, hope holds faith together. Hope gives our faith strength and stability. Some people might say, "Well, what's the difference?" Merriam-webster.com defines hope as cherishing "a desire with anticipation." The same website describes faith as "a firm belief in something for which there is no proof."

Hebrews 11:1 says, *"Now faith is the substance of things hoped for, the evidence of things not seen."* Faith gives MOVEMENT to hope. A person hopes for something and when they begin to act on that hope, faith is born. Let me give you an example: If a person says, "I hope I can lose 30 pounds," and doesn't change their eating habits and doesn't work out, chances are that person is not going to lose the weight. If, however, that person begins to cut back on sweets and makes sure they exercise every day, they will begin to see the evidence of the thing they hoped for!

> *"Even so faith, if it hath not works, is dead, being alone. Yea, a man may say, Thou hast faith, and I have works: shew me thy faith without thy works, and I will shew thee my faith by my works," James 2:17-18.*

The Blood

Oh, the Blood!

Blood is a liquid that travels through the body, delivering nutrients to individual body parts. These nutrients are necessary for the body to "live, move and have it's being" (Acts 17:28).

In Matthew chapter 26, we see Jesus and his disciples preparing to celebrate the Passover. During this celebration, Jesus sent them to secure the place, as an Apostle would. He prophesied to them, as a Prophet would. He went out to minister, as an Evangelist would. He fed them, as a Pastor would. And, He taught them as a teacher would!

Then in verse 27 it says,

> *"And he took the cup, and gave thanks, and gave it to them, saying, Drink ye all of it; for this is my blood of the new testament which is shed for many for the remission of sins."*

The blood represents love.

> *"For God so loved the world, that he gave his only begotten Son, that whosoever believeth in him should not perish, but have everlasting life."*

Why would someone willingly sacrifice his life for someone except he loves them?

The law of God required blood sacrifice for atonement for sin. That sacrifice could only be obtained through death! For hundreds of years, God accepted the blood of animals in exchange for the sinner's blood. But, Jesus paid the ultimate price, and spilled HIS blood in exchange for ours!

Jesus commanded us in Matthew 23:37-38 to love the Lord with all our heart, soul and mind and then to love our

Temple Building: Realigning The Body of Christ

neighbor as ourselves. If we love God, we will do His work on this earth. If we love others, we will be helpful to them, heal them and provide for them as Jesus did.

What does the Bible say about love?

> *"Love is patient, love is kind. It does not envy, it does not boast, it is not proud. It does not dishonor other, it is not self-seeking, it is not easily angered, it keeps no record of wrongs. Love does not delight in evil but rejoices with the truth. It always protects, always trusts, always hopes, always perseveres,"* I Corinthians 1:13 (NIV).

When the body operates in love it will operate with patience, kindness, and peace. The body operating in love will following the calling of God and always seek to help others instead of tearing them down. The body operating in love will work through hard situations and reach its goal.

As it relates to the Body of Christ, faith, hope and love hold the body in correct alignment and keeps the parts of the body connected to that alignment. Once the body is aligned correctly, it can MOVE out into the world, preaching and teaching the Gospel, which is the Great Commission of Jesus (Matthew 28:19 and Mark 16:15).

8
~The Body Re-Aligned~

Ephesians 4:11, *"And he gave some, apostles; and some, prophets; and some evangelists; and some, pastors and teachers; for the perfecting of the saints, for the work of the ministry, for the edifying of the body of Christ."*

The National Osteoporosis Foundation says that alignment refers to "how the head, shoulders, spine, hips, knees and ankles relate and line up with each other." When any one of these parts fall out of line, the whole body falls out of line. But, when those parts align, the body is capable of moving with perfect accuracy to accomplish its goals. Now that we have looked at each gift Jesus gave to the body and how each gift contributes to the appropriate alignment of the body, let's look at the three things need to be in place in order for the Body to achieve alignment.

Temple Building: Realigning The Body of Christ

The first element of alignment is unity. I love the definition of "unity" that merriam-webster.com gives; "the state of being in complete agreement." The body MUST be in agreement about what it's doing, where it's going and how it's going to get there! What happens when you walk in one direction while looking in another? You run into things! The body, in this case, is not in complete agreement! The eyes are looking in one direction, but the body is going somewhere else.

Psalm 133:1-3 says,

> *"Behold, how good and how pleasant it is for brethren to dwell together in unity! ²It is like the precious ointment upon the head that ran down upon the beard even Aaron's beard: that went down to the skirts of his garments."*

Unity is like anointing oil, that when applied to the HEAD, anoints THE WHOLE BODY! When each part of the body appreciates the unique workings of the other parts of the body, unity is achieved.

Now, there can be no pride in a unified body! For pride in one member of the body will take the body out of agreement and cause the whole body to suffer. Paul tells the Galatians in chapter five and verse nine that "a little leaven leaveneth the whole lump." We can see this in the hips often. When the hips are out of line, the upper body is then disconnected from the lower body. The body CAN move with the hips out of line, but the movement will not be very swift and the back will eventually lose strength and be in great pain.

~The Body Re-Aligned~

But Jesus was very plain when He said that if your foot, or hand, or eye offends the body, you should remove that body part so it doesn't affect the whole body, (paraphrasing Mark chapter 9).

This leads me to the next element the body must have to achieve alignment, consecration. Consecration is the process of making someone or something clean and holy unto The Lord. 2 Corinthians 7:1 says, *"Having therefore these promises, dearly beloved, let us cleanse ourselves from all filthiness of the flesh and spirit, perfecting holiness in the fear of God."*

Holiness is not a cult of overzealous, religious nuts! It's a word that means you are set apart for a special purpose. Consecration is an act of repentance from allowing the body to act in ungodly ways, and then acting in holiness. We often quote Romans 12:1, *"…present your bodies a living sacrifice, holy, acceptable unto God, which is your reasonable service."* But, we have to remember that the original sacrifices were to have "no spot or blemish." No spot or blemish means that your body is ONLY used to please God. It means that the body should not be influenced by the world or move is a way that is worldly.

> *"Neither yield ye your members as instruments of unrighteousness unto sin: but yield yourselves unto God, as those that are alive from the dead, and your members as instruments of righteousness unto God,"* Romans 6:13.

Temple Building: Realigning The Body of Christ

That means the Body and its members should exhibit the fruits of the Spirit, not the fruits of the flesh. The fruits of the flesh and the fruits of the Spirit can be found in Galatians chapter 5.

> *"The acts of the flesh are obvious: sexual immorality, impurity and debauchery; idolatry and witchcraft; hatred, discord, jealousy, fits of rage, selfish ambition, dissensions, factions and envy; drunkenness, orgies, and the like. I warn you, as I did before, that those who live like this will not inherit the kingdom of God. But the fruit of the Spirit is love, joy, peace, forbearance, kindness, goodness, faithfulness, gentleness and self-control. Against such things there is no law. Those who belong to Christ Jesus have crucified the flesh with its passions and desires. Since we live by the Spirit, let us keep in step with the Spirit."* Galatians 5:19-25 (NIV).

So examine the body that YOU are a part of. Is it operating in the fruits of the flesh or the Spirit? Are you holding popular exercise classes that perpetuate sexuality and idolatry at your church?! (We will discuss this more in volume 2!) Are couples being allowed to live in sin?! Are leaders making decisions that benefit themselves over the people they serve?! If the answer to any of these questions is "yes," your body needs to be consecrated! Paul says, in Romans 6:23 that the wages of the sins listed above are death! Are you worshiping at a DEAD church, expecting to find a LIVING savior?! Consecrate your body today and receive the gift of God, which is eternal life!

How do we consecrate our body parts? We TRAIN them to do what is right by washing with the Word of God. Too often, church members are dismissed by church leaders when they feel a calling to minister in a charismatic gifting. The word of God gives instructions for each member of the Body to operate in holiness. We as a Body must stop glossing over those "charismatic" scriptures or scriptures that confront hard issues such as idolatry and sexual immorality, and realize that, even though the word was written thousands of years ago, it is still relevant today. A church leader who is not equipped to train the body in a specific area should find training programs for that body part instead of dismissing the calling that may be on that individual's life. When we allow the Holy Spirit to operate freely in the body, the body becomes consecrated.

Once the body is consecrated, we must proceed to the next phase of alignment, obedience. Obedience, in regards to the body, speaks to movement. The only way to move in obedience in God's call for the body is to allow each part to DO its part! This is called EXERCISE!

> *"For as we have many members in one body, and all members have not the same office: So we, being many are one body in Christ, and every one members one of another. Having then gifts differing according to the grace that is given to us, whether prophecy, let us prophesy according to the proportion of faith; or ministry, let us wait on our*

Temple Building: Realigning The Body of Christ

ministering: or he that teacheth, on teaching; Or he that exhorteth, on exhortation: he that giveth, let him do it with simplicity; he that ruleth, with diligence; he that sheweth mercy, with cheerfulness," Romans 12:4-8

Merriam-Webster.com defines exercise as "physical activity that is done in order to become stronger and healthier." Have you ever started an exercise program after being sedentary for a while? It's not easy, is it? You may not be able to do 20 squats to start. You may have to start at 10 squats. However, if you keep challenging yourself to do one more squat each day than the day before, you can work up to that 20 squat goal. The body becomes more fit with every squat you add to your set. But, it takes every part of the body working together to do so.

The first exercise the Body must do is lift Jesus! *"And I, if I be lifted up from the earth, will draw all men unto me,"* John 12:32. When we lift Jesus up as Lord and Savior, when we follow His commandment to "Go," and when we do these things in unity, Jesus will do the rest! Our job as servants of the Lord becomes so much easier when we praise Him!

The next exercise the Body must do is carry each other's burdens. *"Bear ye one another's burdens, and so fulfil the law of Christ,"* Galatians 6:2.

Our mission as the Body of Christ is to GO; be the conduit of love, justice, mercy and grace! We have to be the body that leads the blind body to be healed by Jesus. We have to be the hands that unclog clogged ears. We have to be feet that lead others to walk the path of righteousness.

~The Body Re-Aligned~

We've got to allow the body parts to do what they were created to do. The more the body MOVES the better fit it is *to move*!

So, you see, Christ himself gave the alignment of Apostle to oversee and dispatch the each part of the body as necessary, the Prophet to govern the word of God to the body, the Evangelist to spread the Word, the Pastor to nurture and build the Body, and the Teacher to establish the firm foundation of the Word for the Body to stand on and walk in! When the Five-Fold Ministries are aligned in the Church, faith hope and love are engaged. The Body then filters out the worldly influences and begins to operate in holiness unto the Lord. The rest of the body will then begin to MOVE for the "edifying of the body of Christ!"

Building The Temple

Which part of the Body are YOU?

God has given you a part to play in the Body of Christ. If you are not already operating in the gifts of the Spirit that have been given to you, recommit your gifts to Him today, and allow Him to consecrate those gives in you. If you do not know which body part you are, there are several Spiritual Gifts tests online that you can take which will give you understanding. Read the Bible or take a course to teach you how to work those gifts for God's glory and for the edification of the Body.

Below is an adaptation of the Temple Dedication prayer that Solomon prayed when the Temple was built, including excerpts from Ephesians chapter four and other scriptures referenced in this book. Pray this prayer daily as a declaration that you are the Temple of the Holy Spirit. Church leaders, pray this prayer over your church as a reminder of your collective calling to GO YE THERFORE!

Temple Building: Realigning The Body of Christ

Temple Dedication Prayer

Lord, God of Israel, there is no god like you in heaven above or on earth. Now, Father, I build for you this day, a magnificent Temple for you, unified by faith, a place for you to dwell forever. I declare that THIS BODY is THE TEMPLE of God!

- I declare that I have the mind I Christ. With my ears I will hear the voice of God. With my eyes I will be led by the vision of the Lord. With my nose I will discern His Spirit. And, with my mouth I will speak the truth in love.
- I will carry the Government of knowledge, understanding and wisdom on my shoulders. I will intercede on behalf of those who need You and I will use my hands for Godly works.
- I will sow seeds of righteousness and salvation, and carry the word of God to the nations.
- I will carry the burdens of my neighbor to edify the Body of Christ.
- Help me walk worthy of the calling you have placed on my life, not as the Gentiles walk, with vanity of their minds.

I dedicate this Temple to you today. May what comes in this Temple and what goes out of this Temple honor and glorify you at all times. Search this Temple and if you find anything in there that is not like you remove it NOW! May your eyes be open toward this Temple night and day, this place, of which you said, "My Name shall be there." Hear the supplication of your servant as we pray in this place. Let your glory fill this Temple. I'll give you praise, honor and glory forever.

Amen!

REFERENCES

Goll, James, <u>The Seer: The Prophetic Power of Visions, Dreams and Open Heavens</u>, Destiny Image Publishers, Inc., Shippensburg, 2012.

<u>The Holy Bible,</u> King James Version via The Bible App, Crown Copyright, UK.

<u>The Holy Bible</u>, New International Version via The Bible App, Biblica, Inc., 2011.

Blueletterbible.org

Freebiblestudyguides.org

Healthline.com

Healthpages.org

Innerbody.com

Kidshealth.org

Merriam-webster.com

About the Author

Tfifany Moore Palmer has operated in a heavy prophetic anointing all her life. Growing up in a traditional church setting, that gift was not nurtured and she often felt she had to hide that gift from the church. Her desire to see people worship in complete freedom provided the inspiration for this work.

Tfifany knew at an early age that she was going to be a dancer. She attended the South Carolina Governor's School for the Arts for two years and she obtained a minor in Dance at Winthrop University. Tfifany attended the Alvin Ailey American Dance Center Summer Program in 1996 and the Certificate Program in 1998, where she was called to dance ministry.

In 2011, Tfifany received her dance ministry license from the Eagles International Training Institute (EITI). Currently, she is an international teacher, mentor and motivator as the EITI Dance Year 2 Instructor as well as the Ballet and Modern Instructor for the Eagles International Technique Centre, online dance technique program. Tfifany is the founder of Total Praise Dance Academy located in Aiken, South Carolina, where she resides with her loving husband and two beautiful daughters.

www.ingramcontent.com/pod-product-compliance
Lightning Source LLC
LaVergne TN
LVHW051150080426
835508LV00021B/2571